WILD BACKYARD ANIMALS

Watch Out for
WASPS!

Devon Mckinney

PowerKiDS press.

New York

Published in 2016 by The Rosen Publishing Group, Inc.
29 East 21st Street, New York, NY 10010

First Edition

Editor: Caitlin McAneney
Book Design: Katelyn Heinle/Tanya Dellaccio

Photo Credits: Cover Olga_Phoenix/Shutterstock.com; p. 4 Dancestrokes/Shutterstock.com; p. 5 Nomad_Soul/Shutterstock.com; p. 6 SaraJo/Shutterstock.com; p. 7 Elizabeth A. Cummings/Shutterstock.com; p. 8 (giant hornet) https://en.wikipedia.org/wiki/Asian_giant_hornet#/media/File:Vespa_mandarinia_japonica_IMG_0214.JPG; p. 8 (fairy fly) https://en.wikipedia.org/wiki/Fairyfly#/media/File:Cremnomymar_sp..jpg; p. 9 (ichneumon wasp) Melinda Fawver/Shutterstock.com; p. 9 (yellow jacket) irin-k/Shutterstock.com; p. 10 Tom Grundy/Shutterstock.com; p. 11 Vector3D/Shutterstock.com; p. 12 Stephen Bonk/Shutterstock.com; p. 13 Robert & Jean Pollock/Visuals Unlimited, Inc./Getty Images; p. 15 Richard McManus/Moment Open/Getty Images; p. 16 Shishka4/Shutterstock.com; p. 17 David Peter Ryan/Shutterstock.com; p. 19 Juergen Faelchle/Shutterstock.com; p. 21 Annette Shaff/Shutterstock.com; p. 22 Andrea J. Smith/Shutterstock.com.

Cataloging-in-Publication Data

Names: McKinney, Devon.
Title: Watch out for wasps! / Devon McKinney.
Description: New York : PowerKids Press, 2016. | Series: Wild backyard animals | Includes index.
Identifiers: ISBN 9781508142706 (pbk.) | ISBN 9781508142812 (6 pack) | ISBN 9781508142829 (library bound)
Subjects: LCSH: Wasps–Juvenile literature.
Classification: LCC QL565.2 M43 2016 | DDC 595.79'8–dc23

Manufactured in the United States of America

CPSIA Compliance Information: Batch #BW16PK: For Further Information contact Rosen Publishing, New York, New York at 1-800-237-9932

CONTENTS

OUCH, THAT STINGS!

Imagine you're having a picnic outside when suddenly you feel a sharp sting on your arm. You see a black-and-yellow bug fly away, and then you know—you've been stung by a wasp.

There are many kinds of wasps, but the ones you'll most often find in your backyard are yellow jackets and hornets. These bugs look a bit like bees, but don't be mistaken. Wasps are more likely to give a painful sting!

HONEYBEE

BACKYARD BITES
You might mistake a wasp for a honeybee. Many wasps have black and yellow stripes. Read on to find out how to tell them apart!

SOME PEOPLE ARE **ALLERGIC** TO WASP **VENOM.** IT'S VERY IMPORTANT FOR THEM TO WATCH OUT FOR WASPS.

MANY WASP SPECIES

There are around 30,000 species, or kinds, of wasps that we know about. They live all over the world. In fact, they're found nearly everywhere except Antarctica.

You may be familiar with yellow jackets and hornets because they live in large groups. However, wasps come in many different sizes, shapes, and colors. Some are even blue, brown, or red. The largest wasps are usually hard to find because they don't live in big groups and usually don't sting people.

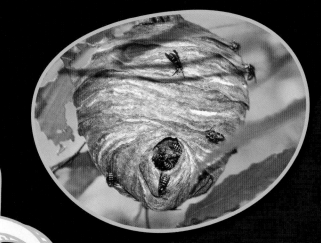

BACKYARD BITES

There are two major kinds of wasps: solitary and social. Social wasps live in large communities called colonies. Solitary wasps usually keep away from people and prefer to hunt alone.

THIS TARANTULA HAWK WASP IS A SOLITARY WASP. THE HORNETS ON PAGE SIX ARE SOCIAL WASPS.

IDENTIFYING A WASP

How can you tell a wasp apart from other flying bugs in your backyard? They have several **identifying** features that set them apart from other bugs.

All wasps have two pairs of wings. Their bodies are separated into three segments, or parts: the head, thorax, and abdomen. Unlike honeybees, wasps have a "pinched" waist, which separates the thorax and abdomen. Only female wasps have a stinger. These stingers **evolved** from body parts that used to lay eggs, called ovipositors.

FAIRY WASP

ASIAN GIANT HORNET

BACKYARD BITES

The smallest wasps, known as fairy wasps, only grow up to 0.04 inch (1 mm) long. The largest social wasps, called Asian giant hornets, can grow to be more than 2 inches (5 cm) long.

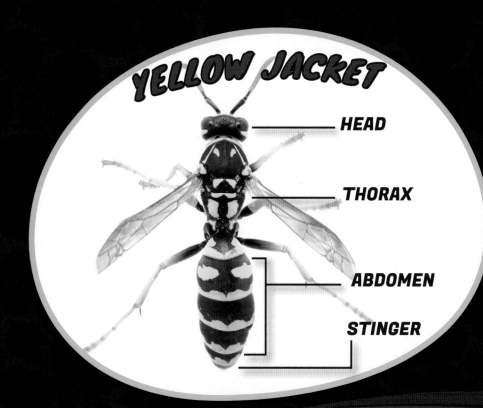

YELLOW JACKET

HEAD

THORAX

ABDOMEN

STINGER

ICHNEUMON WASP

OVIPOSITOR

SOME WASPS STILL HAVE OVIPOSITORS AND USE THEM TO LAY EGGS. THIS IS AN ICHNEUMON WASP. HER OVIPOSITOR HELPS HER LAY EGGS INTO WOOD.

INSIDE A WASP NEST

Queen wasps spend winter in a warm hideout. This could be a hollow tree, or a shed in your backyard. In the spring, the queen leaves her hideout. She builds a small nest and cares for a group of worker wasps. The worker females start building on to the nest. Each tiny section, or cell, of the nest has six sides. It's the queen's job to lay eggs in the nest.

When late summer comes, the nest is buzzing with activity. Most social wasps build large nests each year that can house more than 5,000 wasps. You might find a buzzing nest in a tree in your backyard or even on your house!

BACKYARD BITES

When the weather gets cold, most wasps die, and the nests are left behind.

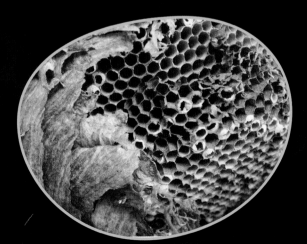

PAPER WASPS MAKE THEIR NESTS BY CHEWING PLANT MATTER AND SPITTING IT OUT. IT FORMS MATERIAL THAT LOOKS LIKE PAPER.

A WASP'S DIET

You've probably seen wasps buzzing around your plate at a picnic or even flying over trash. What are they trying to eat?

Most wasps eat nectar—a sweet, sticky liquid in flowers. Others may eat fruit, too. If you have something sweet on your plate, a wasp may be interested in taking a bite. Wasps can also be frightening predators. They use the venom in their sting to **paralyze** their **prey**. Then they bring food back to their larvae, or baby wasps.

SOME WASPS ARE PARASITIC, MEANING THEY LIVE OFF OTHER ANIMALS IN A HARMFUL WAY. THEY USE THEIR OVIPOSITORS TO LAY EGGS INSIDE A BUG. THEN, THEIR LARVAE EAT THE BUG FROM THE INSIDE OUT.

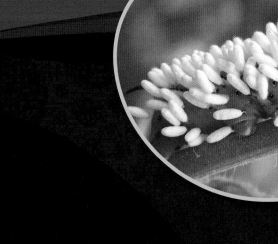

BACKYARD BITES

Western yellow jackets are scavengers, which means they eat nearly anything they can find. They'll look for dead bugs, worms, and even trash.

A STINGING DEFENSE

You might not be afraid to stomp on an anthill or swipe a spider web. But you sure don't want to mess with a wasp nest! That's because of the wasp's ability to sting—a **defense** that keeps it safe.

If a social wasp feels unsafe, it releases a **chemical** that other wasps pick up on. They come together in a big group and then sting their enemy. They also use their sting to paralyze small prey.

WASP VENOM HAS A CHEMICAL THAT BREAKS DOWN CELL WALLS. IT ALSO MAKES SOME PEOPLES' BODIES RELEASE HISTAMINE, WHICH CAUSES SYMPTOMS, OR SIGNS, OF AN ALLERGY, SUCH AS DIZZINESS AND TROUBLE BREATHING.

A WASP'S LIFE

Most wasps begin their life inside a six-sided cell in a nest. A queen wasp can lay around 100 eggs per day. She lays eggs in spring and early summer. Many of them **develop** into worker wasps that build the nest and gather food.

At the end of the summer, a queen lays queen eggs and drone eggs. Queen eggs grow into wasps with the ability to have babies, and they may develop into a queen. Other eggs grow into wasps that can't have babies, and they turn into males, or drones, that can **mate** with the potential queen.

AFTER HATCHING FROM THEIR EGGS, WASP LARVAE WILL BE FED DEAD INSECTS. OVER TIME, THEY GROW WINGS SO THEY CAN LEAVE THE NEST IN SEARCH OF FOOD.

BACKYARD BITES

Queen wasps are easily identified because they often grow much bigger than other wasps in the nest. If you search your shed in the winter, you may find a sleeping queen.

MORE THAN A STING

If a wasp stings you, you'll probably feel a painful pinch. Most people may have swelling near the spot. However, some people can have a very bad allergic reaction.

Some symptoms of an allergic reaction are swelling of the throat, lips, and mouth. A person may throw up or feel sick to their stomach. Some may have trouble breathing or even pass out. Some develop an itchy rash on their skin called hives. Some people even have to go to the hospital after a wasp sting.

People can be allergic to wasps, but not to bees. It's important to know what you're allergic to so you can avoid those buzzing beasts.

IF YOU'RE STUNG BY A WASP, YOU CAN TAKE A DRUG CALLED AN ANTIHISTAMINE. IT STOPS ALLERGY SYMPTOMS FROM STARTING. CLEAN THE SPOT WHERE YOU WERE STUNG AND PUT ICE ON IT UNTIL THE SWELLING GOES DOWN.

STAYING SAFE

The most common backyard wasps are yellow jackets. They may swarm around you if you have food out. To keep yellow jackets away, make sure you don't leave food or trash out. You can buy special sprays to keep wasps away. Some people set special traps to catch wasps.

If you have a nest near your house, you may need to have it removed. It's important to have this done by a professional exterminator, or a person who gets rid of pests, because it's very **dangerous**.

BACKYARD BITES

Hornet nests are very dangerous. People who try to remove them should wear a wasp suit, which is sealed at the ankles, wrists, and collar.

REMOVING A NEST OR SPRAYING FOR WASPS SHOULD BE DONE AT NIGHT BECAUSE THE WASPS ARE ALL IN THE NEST.

WONDERFUL WASPS?

Wasps aren't all bad. In fact, farmers can use parasitic wasps to kill bugs that feast on their crops. Many wasps also **pollinate** plants that grow around the world. Scientists are even looking into ways that the venom of a Brazilian wasp can help fight cancer.

If you see a wasp, it's best to let it go on its way. Next time you see a familiar yellow jacket in your backyard, think of all the other wonderful wasp species!

GLOSSARY

allergic: Having a bad bodily reaction to certain foods, animals, or surroundings.

chemical: Matter that can be mixed with other matter to cause changes.

dangerous: Unsafe.

defense: A feature of a living thing that helps keep it safe.

develop: To go through a process of natural growth and change.

evolve: To grow and change over time.

identify: To tell what something is.

mate: To come together to make babies.

material: Something used to make something else.

paralyze: To make something unable to move.

pollinate: To take pollen from one flower, plant, or tree to another.

prey: An animal hunted by other animals for food.

venom: A type of poison made by an animal and passed to another animal by a sting or bite.

INDEX

WEBSITES

Due to the changing nature of Internet links, PowerKids Press has developed
an online list of websites related to the subject of this book. This site is updated
regularly. Please use this link to access the list: www.powerkidslinks.com/wba/wasp